Freelance Writing

For Greeting Card Companies

by

Patrisha Stauss

dp
DISTINCTIVE PUBLISHING CORP.

Freelance Writing for Greeting Card Companies
By Patrisha Stauss
Copyright 1993 by Patrisha Stauss

Published by Distinctive Publishing Corp.
P.O. Box 17868
Plantation, Florida 33318-7868
Printed in the United States of America

ISBN: 0-942963-26-1
Library of Congress No.: 92-17088
Price: $9.95

Library of Congress Cataloging-in-Publication Data

Stauss, Patrisha, 1955 -
    Freelance writing for greeting card companies / by Patrisha Stauss.
        p.   cm.
    Includes index.
    ISBN 0-942963-26-1 : $9.95
    1. Greeting cards—Authorship. 2. Authorship I. Title.
PN171.G74S7   1992
808'.066811—dc20   92-17088
                                                            CIP

Are thoughts enough to take you
where you wish to go?
Well, I guess if you don't try them out,
you will never know.

This and all enclosed passages by Ronny B.

TABLE OF CONTENTS

INTRODUCTION

This book has been written to show a writer how to enter the greeting card market. You will be taken step-by-step through the process of professionally preparing yourself and your material to be reviewed by editors at card companies. Several different businesses will use verses or passages for their products. When appropriate, a few details in those areas will be discussed.

Writing is a good form of self-expression. What better place to have your writing appear than in greeting cards? With this genre, you are expressing your own thoughts at the same time you are helping others express how they feel. This is possible because many find it difficult to say what they feel, and they will buy a greeting card to speak for them.

Having your material reviewed by card companies will be easier than having your work accepted and bought by them. Depending on your experience, this book will help in one or more of the following areas: knowing the business of writing, learning the process of approaching greeting card companies, motivating yourself to write verses or passages, improving your organizational skills, knowing your rights as a writer, and preparing your other written material for resale. Remember that if you make your work original, unique and eye-catching, you will increase your chances of having your material on the market.

If you have written material in the form of poetry, passages, thoughts or verses, you will be able to use them for greeting card companies or other product lines.

Some photographs or illustrations can be used, with or without your written work, to enhance your chances of grabbing an editor's attention.

By the time you finish reading this book, you should be more aware of the process of contacting agencies, publishers and editors. You will know how to get and stay organized and be able to professionally prepare your ideas for sale on the market.

THE BUSINESS OF WRITING

Whether you freelance part-time or full-time, you must be prepared to invest some time in managing your business. It takes more than writing skill for you to be efficient and successful. To give yourself a positive edge over other writers, you must learn to plan your time, stay organized, be critical of your work, and remain aware of the pros and cons of trying to get into the greeting card business.

As a serious freelance writer, you should take a professional approach, a process more specifically considered in Section Three. In order to look and be professional you must plan to invest some money in one or more of the items below:

computer hardware	camera equipment
computer software	camera supplies
electric typewriter	artist's material

As a computer owner, you can count on investing in paper, ink cartridges, computer repairs, word processing software, floppy disks, and possibly, font cartridges, graphics software, and a mouse and pad.

As a typewriter owner, you must invest in paper, ink ribbons, correctional tape, and repairs.

Camera equipment requires spending money on the camera, film (processing and developing it), lenses, filters, a carrying case, and preparing or searching for the photo shoot.

Illustrators will need to invest in art paper, drawing (coloring) utensils or paint, canvas, and other miscellaneous items.

Regardless of what your decision is about the above items, you will have to invest in the following:

paper	pencils/pens	research books
pencil sharpener	erasers	stamps
envelopes	dictionary	address research
photocopying cost	paper clips	telephone costs

An investment of time is also essential. You need to research and get to know what kind of cards are sold on the market so that you will know which companies fit your style of writing. For example, if you like to write humorous verses, then you should research that area of the market. Be aware of your competition. The more aware you are, the more you will be able to produce the quality of work which an editor would like to see. When you look at the cards already on the market, be as critical as you think an editor would be. In fact, you should judge your work (whether a written verse or passage, a photograph, or an illustration) with the same critical eye. Further consideration of this topic can be found in Section Three.

Before you send your material to a publisher or an editor, you should copyright and register it. The copyright law will protect your work and officially recognize you as its owner and creator. It endows you with the benefits and privileges which ownership entails, and it establishes the fact that only you can decide how the work is to be used, unless you sell that right. The copyright law gives you particular power in dealing with anyone who wants to market your material. You should understand fully how to use this power so that you will not lose your ownership.

It is easy to copyright your material, but there are many aspects of the law; you should be aware of all these areas. The more knowledge you have about your rights as owner of your work, the less frustrated you will be if a particular issue arises.

If you do not register your work before submitting it, you can do so within five years of its publication. I advise you to register the work first, for your protection.

No matter what you send and to whom you send it, do it in a business-like fashion. Think about how you would like to receive material; in other words, think as an editor does.

It's obvious that you need an address before you send your material. Not so obvious is the fact that you need a query letter. This is a brief, yet specific, letter stating that you would like permission to send your material to the company for review. Within the letter you should ask for writer's, photographer's, and/or illustrator's guidelines. The purpose of this is for your benefit; you want to send material which the card company can sell.

If possible, the address on the letter should consist of an "Attention" line stating the name of who is to receive the letter. Be sure you have the correct ZIP code on the envelope.

If you can't interest the editor, you may get a rejection notice in the mail. You can expect to receive many "rejection" or "not interested" notices for various reasons. Your submission may be turned down because it does not suit the editor's personality, or the work load of the company is too heavy to take on more material, or your subject matter may not fit the company's needs. There are many such reasons over which you have little control.

Don't get frustrated to the point of giving up writing. You must develop the patience and allow yourself enough time to successfully pursue this avenue of freelance writing.

The Market

The greeting card market is highly competitive; your style must be unique, but not off-beat. In order for you to be competitive with your material, you should familiarize yourself with the type of card company that fits your style. The best place to research card company material is at any store which has a high volume of customers. You can look in the smaller stores, but you will find a greater variety of cards in larger stores.

When you research the market, pay attention to current topics, artwork or photographs, size and shape of cards, and prices. It's important to know these areas for the following reasons:

1. **Current topics** — If you don't stay within the current trends, the editor you approach may be skeptical of placing your work on the market for fear that few people would buy it. The editor might believe that your submission wouldn't be profitable for the company because the product does not lie within the company's subject realm. It is also possible for your work to be rejected by the editor because you did not follow the company's guidelines with regard to topic(s) and/or style.

2. **Artwork/Photographs** — Although some card companies will take both your writing and your artwork or photographs, they often take only your writing and use it with illustrations or photographs generated by others. Likewise a card company might take your artwork or photographs and add verses created by other writers. These others may be on staff or other freelancers. The only way you can find out what stance the company takes on this subject is by writing for guidelines in all areas. The company will let you know what its expectations are; you need to be aware of the company's preference.

3. **Card size and shape** — If you have a creative imagination for exploring various sizes and shapes of greeting cards, be sure to find out which companies will allow you this

opportunity. If you find a company which specifies size and/or shape and you fit the other categories which are mentioned in the guidelines, submit only what is specified. An editor is likely to return material to those who did not meet the guidelines. Don't take that chance.

4. **Price** — Look at the price of a card in relation to the first three aspects. This will give you an idea of what price your cards may carry. If you're not aware of card prices, you won't be prepared to discuss payment terms appropriately, and you may not know if you can make a profit.

Once you have researched these four areas, you will be ready to write to editors, impressing them with your work by fitting into their company's styles. First, you should send a query letter requesting guidelines. These will be quite specific. If you do not see a reference to your style in the guidelines of a particular company, you may disregard sending your material there. However, if you believe strongly in some particular work, you may write back and ask the editor if she/he would consider reviewing your material.

Before you send your work to anyone, for any reason, you should take the steps described below.

Copyright/Register Your Work

As previously mentioned, the copyright law will protect your work and recognize you as the owner and creator. You will have the benefits and privileges that ownership entails. Minors may claim a copyright, but state laws may regulate their business dealings. For further information regarding minors and the state laws, write to the Copyright Office.

What is a copyright? The current copyright law has been in effect since January 1, 1978. The law was established to protect the work of the creator; it states that the creator is its owner. As owner, you are empowered to say how your work is to be used and by whom. The law gives the owner power in dealing with editors, publishers and anyone else who may want to purchase or use the copyrighted work. As owner you can authorize others to:

- reproduce the work;
- prepare derivative works based upon the original;
- distribute copies for rental, lease or lending; and
- display the work publicly.

You do not have to register your work with the Copyright Office to show legal ownership. If you do register your work, you will have certain advantages beyond just the show of copyright. You must register the work before you can go to court in a dispute over rights or ownership. With registration, you can sue for statutory damages and, in addition, recover attorney fees. A registered copyright gives you a stronger case when in court, because you have definite proof of your ownership.

If you want to transfer your copyright, it must be stated in writing in order to be valid. If you do this, you lose all your rights to the material or work. If a company will not offer to retransfer your rights, you can get them back by serving a written notice forty years after the transfer was made. If the work was published, you can get back the rights thirty-five years after the publication date. Consult the Copyright Office for further information on this issue.

A copyright is subject to the various state laws and regulations governing ownership, inheritance and transfer of personal property. For information about relevant state laws, you should consult an attorney.

What can be copyrighted? Copyright protection exists for original works when they become a form of expression, as long as they can be communicated in written, visual or audio records. Copyrighted works include:

- literary works;
- musical works, including words;
- dramatic works, including music;
- pictorial, graphic and sculptural works;
- motion pictures and other audio visual works; and
- sound recordings.

These are broad categories which consist of subcategories. For the purpose of this book we will cover the areas of literary and pictorial works.

The following categories of material cannot be copyrighted:

- speeches which have not been written;
- titles, names, short phrases and slogans, lettering, coloring, or word and content lists;
- ideas, procedures, methods, systems, processes, concepts, principles, discoveries or explanations;
- works of information that are common property for everyone (*e.g.*, calendars, appointment books, and any lists or tables taken from public documents).

How to copyright/register your work. You can copyright your work with or without registering with the Copyright Office. You can personally copyright your work with one of the following notations:

- Copyright P. Stauss 1992
- Copr. P. Stauss 1992
- © P. Stauss 1992

Some variations are:

- positions of date and name may be reversed;
- date of completion or year of first publication can be omitted if a pictorial or graphic work accompanies text and is reproduced in or on greeting cards, postcards or stationery; and
- name of the owner can be a full name, an abbreviation or a generally known alternative designation of the owner.

Display of a copyright notice is especially important if you add your work to another work which has not been copyrighted. Not having a copyright notice may result in another's trying to claim ownership of your work. You should make it a habit to place the copyright notice on all your unpublished work. No matter how you decide to display your copyright notice, be consistent, so that your work isn't likely to be disputed.

Unlike the Copyright Law before 1978, the current law provides a procedure for correcting errors and omissions on copyright notices for published and unpublished works. The omission or error does not automatically invalidate the copyright if the registration for the work has been made before or within five years after publication date. A reasonable effort has to be made to correct the error after it has been discovered. Write to the Copyright Office for further information in this area.

If you send any of your work overseas, you need specific information. To receive details about what you need for international copyright protection, write to the Copyright Office.

For a small fee, you may obtain more protection by registering your work with the Copyright Office. In general, the copyright registration is a legal formality which establishes a public record and assists in any court matters over ownership.

When you write to the Register of Copyrights, ask for the current fee and the following application forms:

Form TX: for literary works, non-dramatic

Form SE: for literary works that would be used in such periodicals as newspapers, magazines, newsletters, and journals

Form VA: for visual arts: pictorial, graphic, and sculptural

Form CA: to correct or change information sent on an earlier registration form to the Copyright Office

To register your work, write to:

Register of Copyrights
Library of Congress
Washington DC 20559

When you register your work with the Copyright Office, you need to send the correct form completely filled out, one copy of the finished work if unpublished (two copies if it is published), and the current fee requested by the office.

Following are examples of the forms mentioned above. When the forms are sent to you, a pamphlet of instructions will accompany each one.

FORM TX
For a Literary Work
UNITED STATES COPYRIGHT OFFICE

REGISTRATION NUMBER

| TX | TXU |

EFFECTIVE DATE OF REGISTRATION

| Month | Day | Year |

DO NOT WRITE ABOVE THIS LINE. IF YOU NEED MORE SPACE, USE A SEPARATE CONTINUATION SHEET.

1 TITLE OF THIS WORK ▼

PREVIOUS OR ALTERNATIVE TITLES ▼

PUBLICATION AS A CONTRIBUTION If this work was published as a contribution to a periodical, serial, or collection, give information about the collective work in which the contribution appeared. Title of Collective Work ▼

If published in a periodical or serial give: Volume ▼   Number ▼   Issue Date ▼   On Pages ▼

2 NAME OF AUTHOR ▼

DATES OF BIRTH AND DEATH
Year Born ▼   Year Died ▼

Was this contribution to the work a "work made for hire"?
☐ Yes
☐ No

AUTHOR'S NATIONALITY OR DOMICILE
Name of Country
OR { Citizen of ▶
Domiciled in ▶

WAS THIS AUTHOR'S CONTRIBUTION TO THE WORK
Anonymous?   ☐ Yes ☐ No
Pseudonymous?   ☐ Yes ☐ No
If the answer to either of these questions is "Yes," see detailed instructions.

NOTE
Under the law, the "author" of a "work made for hire" is generally the employer, not the employee (see instructions). For any part of this work that was "made for hire" check "Yes" in the space provided, give the employer (or other person for whom the work was prepared) as "Author" of that part, and leave the space for dates of birth and death blank.

NATURE OF AUTHORSHIP Briefly describe nature of the material created by this author in which copyright is claimed. ▼

NAME OF AUTHOR ▼

DATES OF BIRTH AND DEATH
Year Born ▼   Year Died ▼

Was this contribution to the work a "work made for hire"?
☐ Yes
☐ No

AUTHOR'S NATIONALITY OR DOMICILE
Name of Country
OR { Citizen of ▶
Domiciled in ▶

WAS THIS AUTHOR'S CONTRIBUTION TO THE WORK
Anonymous?   ☐ Yes ☐ No
Pseudonymous?   ☐ Yes ☐ No
If the answer to either of these questions is "Yes," see detailed instructions.

NATURE OF AUTHORSHIP Briefly describe nature of the material created by this author in which copyright is claimed. ▼

NAME OF AUTHOR ▼

DATES OF BIRTH AND DEATH
Year Born ▼   Year Died ▼

Was this contribution to the work a "work made for hire"?
☐ Yes
☐ No

AUTHOR'S NATIONALITY OR DOMICILE
Name of Country
OR { Citizen of ▶
Domiciled in ▶

WAS THIS AUTHOR'S CONTRIBUTION TO THE WORK
Anonymous?   ☐ Yes ☐ No
Pseudonymous?   ☐ Yes ☐ No
If the answer to either of these questions is "Yes," see detailed instructions.

NATURE OF AUTHORSHIP Briefly describe nature of the material created by this author in which copyright is claimed. ▼

3 YEAR IN WHICH CREATION OF THIS WORK WAS COMPLETED This information must be given in all cases.
◀ Year

DATE AND NATION OF FIRST PUBLICATION OF THIS PARTICULAR WORK
Complete this information ONLY if this work has been published.
Month ▶   Day ▶   Year ▶
◀ Nation

4 COPYRIGHT CLAIMANT(S) Name and address must be given even if the claimant is the same as the author given in space 2.▼

See instructions before completing this space.

TRANSFER If the claimant(s) named here in space 4 are different from the author(s) named in space 2, give a brief statement of how the claimant(s) obtained ownership of the copyright.▼

APPLICATION RECEIVED

ONE DEPOSIT RECEIVED

TWO DEPOSITS RECEIVED

REMITTANCE NUMBER AND DATE

DO NOT WRITE HERE
OFFICE USE ONLY

MORE ON BACK ▶ • Complete all applicable spaces (numbers 5-11) on the reverse side of this page.
• See detailed instructions.   • Sign the form at line 10.

DO NOT WRITE HERE

EXAMINED BY _____

FORM TX

CHECKED BY _____

☐ CORRESPONDENCE
Yes

FOR
COPYRIGHT
OFFICE
USE
ONLY

DO NOT WRITE ABOVE THIS LINE. IF YOU NEED MORE SPACE, USE A SEPARATE CONTINUATION SHEET.

PREVIOUS REGISTRATION Has registration for this work, or for an earlier version of this work, already been made in the Copyright Office?

☐ Yes ☐ No If your answer is "Yes," why is another registration being sought? (Check appropriate box) ▼

a. ☐ This is the first published edition of a work previously registered in unpublished form.

b. ☐ This is the first application submitted by this author as copyright claimant.

c. ☐ This is a changed version of the work, as shown by space 6 on this application.

If your answer is "Yes," give: **Previous Registration Number** ▼   **Year of Registration** ▼

5

DERIVATIVE WORK OR COMPILATION Complete both space 6a & 6b for a derivative work; complete only 6b for a compilation.

a. **Preexisting Material** Identify any preexisting work or works that this work is based on or incorporates. ▼

b. **Material Added to This Work** Give a brief, general statement of the material that has been added to this work and in which copyright is claimed. ▼

6

See instructions
before completing
this space

—space deleted—

7

REPRODUCTION FOR USE OF BLIND OR PHYSICALLY HANDICAPPED INDIVIDUALS   A signature on this form at space 10, and a
check in one of the boxes here in space 8, constitutes a non-exclusive grant of permission to the Library of Congress to reproduce and distribute solely for the blind
and physically handicapped and under the conditions and limitations prescribed by the regulations of the Copyright Office: (1) copies of the work identified in space
1 of this application in Braille (or similar tactile symbols); or (2) phonorecords embodying a fixation of a reading of that work; or (3) both.

a ☐ Copies and Phonorecords   b ☐ Copies Only   c ☐ Phonorecords Only

8

See instructions

DEPOSIT ACCOUNT If the registration fee is to be charged to a Deposit Account established in the Copyright Office, give name and number of Account.

Name ▼   **Account Number** ▼

9

CORRESPONDENCE Give name and address to which correspondence about this application should be sent   Name/Address/Apt/City/State/Zip ▼

Area Code & Telephone Number ▶

Be sure to
give your
daytime phone
◀ number

CERTIFICATION* I, the undersigned, hereby certify that I am the

Check one ▶

☐ author
☐ other copyright claimant
☐ owner of exclusive right(s)
☐ authorized agent of _____

Name of author or other copyright claimant, or owner of exclusive right(s) ▲

of the work identified in this application and that the statements made
by me in this application are correct to the best of my knowledge.

Typed or printed name and date ▼ If this application gives a date of publication in space 3, do not sign and submit it before that date.

_____ date ▶ _____

Handwritten signature (X) ▼

10

MAIL CERTIFI-CATE TO

Name ▼

Number/Street/Apartment Number ▼

City/State/ZIP ▼

Certificate
will be
mailed in
window
envelope

YOU MUST:
• Complete all necessary spaces
• Sign your application in space 10

**SEND ALL 3 ELEMENTS
IN THE SAME PACKAGE**
1. Application form
2. Nonrefundable $20 filing fee
   in check or money order
   payable to Register of Copyrights
3. Deposit material

MAIL TO:
Register of Copyrights
Library of Congress
Washington, D.C. 20559

11

Copyright fees are ad-
justed at 5-year inter-
vals, based on in-
creases or decreases in
the Consumer Price In-
dex. The next adjust-
ment is due in 1995.
Contact the Copyright
Office in January 1995
for the new fee sched-
ule.

* 17 U.S.C. § 506(e): Any person who knowingly makes a false representation of a material fact in the application for copyright registration provided for by section 409, or in any written statement filed in
connection with the application, shall be fined not more than $2,500.

June 1992—100,000   ☆ U.S. GOVERNMENT PRINTING OFFICE: 1992-312-432/60,004

FORM SE

UNITED STATES COPYRIGHT OFFICE

REGISTRATION NUMBER

EFFECTIVE DATE OF REGISTRATION

Month   Day   Year

DO NOT WRITE ABOVE THIS LINE. IF YOU NEED MORE SPACE, USE A SEPARATE CONTINUATION SHEET.

1   **TITLE OF THIS SERIAL ▼**

Volume ▼   Number ▼   Date on Copies ▼   Frequency of Publication ▼

PREVIOUS OR ALTERNATIVE TITLES ▼

2   **NAME OF AUTHOR ▼**

DATES OF BIRTH AND DEATH ▼
Year Born ▼   Year Died ▼

Was this contribution to the work a "work made for hire"?
☐ Yes
☐ No

AUTHOR'S NATIONALITY OR DOMICILE
Name of Country
OR ☐ Citizen of ▶ _____
☐ Domiciled in ▶ _____

WAS THIS AUTHOR'S CONTRIBUTION TO THE WORK
Anonymous? ☐ Yes ☐ No
Pseudonymous? ☐ Yes ☐ No
If the answer to either of these questions is "Yes," see detailed instructions

NATURE OF AUTHORSHIP   Briefly describe nature of the material created by this author in which copyright is claimed. ▼
☐ Collective Work   Other

NOTE

Under the law the "author" of a "work made for hire" is generally the employer, not the employee (see instructions). For any part of this work that was "made for hire" check "Yes" in the space provided, give the employer (or other person for whom the work was prepared) as "Author" of that part, and leave the space for dates of birth and death blank.

NAME OF AUTHOR ▼

DATES OF BIRTH AND DEATH
Year Born ▼   Year Died ▼

Was this contribution to the work a "work made for hire"?
☐ Yes
☐ No

AUTHOR'S NATIONALITY OR DOMICILE
Name of country
OR ☐ Citizen of ▶ _____
☐ Domiciled in ▶ _____

WAS THIS AUTHOR'S CONTRIBUTION TO THE WORK
Anonymous? ☐ Yes ☐ No
Pseudonymous? ☐ Yes ☐ No
If the answer to either of these questions is "Yes," see detailed instructions

NATURE OF AUTHORSHIP   Briefly describe nature of the material created by this author in which copyright is claimed. ▼
☐ Collective Work   Other

NAME OF AUTHOR ▼

DATES OF BIRTH AND DEATH
Year Born ▼   Year Died ▼

Was this contribution to the work a "work made for hire"?
☐ Yes
☐ No

AUTHOR'S NATIONALITY OR DOMICILE
Name of Country
OR ☐ Citizen of ▶ _____
☐ Domiciled in ▶ _____

WAS THIS AUTHOR'S CONTRIBUTION TO THE WORK
Anonymous? ☐ Yes ☐ No
Pseudonymous? ☐ Yes ☐ No
If the answer to either of these questions is "Yes," see detailed instructions

NATURE OF AUTHORSHIP   Briefly describe nature of the material created by this author in which copyright is claimed. ▼
☐ Collective Work   Other

3   **YEAR IN WHICH CREATION OF THIS ISSUE WAS COMPLETED** This information must be given ◀ Year in all cases.

DATE AND NATION OF FIRST PUBLICATION OF THIS PARTICULAR ISSUE
Complete this information ONLY if this work has been published. Month ▶ _____ Day ▶ _____ Year ▶ _____ ◀ Nation

4   **COPYRIGHT CLAIMANT(S)** Name and address must be given even if the claimant is the same as the author given in space 2.▼

APPLICATION RECEIVED
ONE DEPOSIT RECEIVED
TWO DEPOSITS RECEIVED
REMITTANCE NUMBER AND DATE

DO NOT WRITE HERE — OFFICE USE ONLY

See instructions before completing this space

TRANSFER If the claimant(s) named here in space 4 are different from the author(s) named in space 2, give a brief statement of how the claimant(s) obtained ownership of the copyright ▼

MORE ON BACK ▶ • Complete all applicable spaces (numbers 5-11) on the reverse side of this page
• See detailed instructions   • Sign the form at line 10

DO NOT WRITE HERE
Page 1 of _____ pages

EXAMINED BY

CHECKED BY

☐ CORRESPONDENCE
Yes

FORM SE

FOR
COPYRIGHT
OFFICE
USE
ONLY

DO NOT WRITE ABOVE THIS LINE. IF YOU NEED MORE SPACE, USE A SEPARATE CONTINUATION SHEET.

PREVIOUS REGISTRATION Has registration for this issue, or for an earlier version of this particular issue, already been made in the Copyright Office?

☐ Yes ☐ No If your answer is "Yes," why is another registration being sought? (Check appropriate box) ▼

a. ☐ This is the first published version of an issue previously registered in unpublished form.

b. ☐ This is the first application submitted by this author as copyright claimant.

c. ☐ This is a changed version of this issue, as shown by space 6 on this application.

If your answer is "Yes," give: **Previous Registration Number ▼**　　　**Year of Registration ▼**

5

DERIVATIVE WORK OR COMPILATION Complete both space 6a & 6b for a derivative work; complete only 6b for a compilation.

a. **Preexisting Material** Identify any preexisting work or works that this work is based on or incorporates. ▼

b. **Material Added to This Work** Give a brief, general statement of the material that has been added to this work and in which copyright is claimed. ▼

See instructions
before completing
this space

6

—space deleted—

7

REPRODUCTION FOR USE OF BLIND OR PHYSICALLY HANDICAPPED INDIVIDUALS A signature on this form at space 10, and a check in one of the boxes here in space 8, constitutes a non-exclusive grant of permission to the Library of Congress to reproduce and distribute solely for the blind and physically handicapped and under the conditions and limitations prescribed by the regulations of the Copyright Office: (1) copies of the work identified in space 1 of this application in Braille (or similar tactile symbols); or (2) phonorecords embodying a fixation of a reading of that work; or (3) both.

a ☐ Copies and Phonorecords　　b ☐ Copies Only　　c ☐ Phonorecords Only

See instructions

8

DEPOSIT ACCOUNT If the registration fee is to be charged to a Deposit Account established in the Copyright Office, give name and number of Account.
Name ▼　　　　**Account Number ▼**

9

CORRESPONDENCE Give name and address to which correspondence about this application should be sent. Name Address Apt City State Zip ▼

Area Code & Telephone Number ▶

Be sure to
give your
daytime phone
◀ number

CERTIFICATION* I, the undersigned, hereby certify that I am the
Check one ▶
☐ author
☐ other copyright claimant
☐ owner of exclusive right(s)
☐ authorized agent of

of the work identified in this application and that the statements made by me in this application are correct to the best of my knowledge.

Name of author or other copyright claimant, or owner of exclusive right(s) ▲

Typed or printed name and date ▼ If this application gives a date of publication in space 3, do not sign and submit it before that date.

date ▶

Handwritten signature (X) ▼

10

MAIL CERTIFI-CATE TO

Name ▼

Number Street Apartment Number ▼

City State ZIP ▼

Certificate will be mailed in window envelope

• Complete all necessary spaces
• Sign your application in space 10

SEND ALL 3 ELEMENTS
IN THE SAME PACKAGE
1 Application form
2. Nonrefundable $20 filing fee
in check or money order
payable to Register of Copyrights
3. Deposit material

MAIL TO
Register of Copyrights
Library of Congress
Washington, D.C. 20559

11

* 17 U.S.C. § 506(e) Any person who knowingly makes a false representation of a material fact in the application for copyright registration provided for by section 409, or in any written statement filed in connection with the application, shall be fined not more than $2,500.

▲ February 1991—50,000

☆U.S. GOVERNMENT PRINTING OFFICE: 1991- 282-170/20,013

FORM VA

UNITED STATES COPYRIGHT OFFICE

REGISTRATION NUMBER

VA   VAU

EFFECTIVE DATE OF REGISTRATION

Month   Day   Year

DO NOT WRITE ABOVE THIS LINE. IF YOU NEED MORE SPACE, USE A SEPARATE CONTINUATION SHEET.

1

TITLE OF THIS WORK ▼

NATURE OF THIS WORK ▼ See instructions

PREVIOUS OR ALTERNATIVE TITLES ▼

PUBLICATION AS A CONTRIBUTION If this work was published as a contribution to a periodical, serial, or collection, give information about the collective work in which the contribution appeared.   Title of Collective Work ▼

If published in a periodical or serial give: Volume ▼   Number ▼   Issue Date ▼   On Pages ▼

2 **a**

NAME OF AUTHOR ▼

DATES OF BIRTH AND DEATH
Year Born ▼ Year Died ▼

Was this contribution to the work a "work made for hire"?
☐ Yes
☐ No

AUTHOR'S NATIONALITY OR DOMICILE
Name of Country
OR { Citizen of ▶_____
     { Domiciled in ▶_____

WAS THIS AUTHOR'S CONTRIBUTION TO THE WORK
Anonymous?   ☐ Yes ☐ No
Pseudonymous? ☐ Yes ☐ No

If the answer to either of these questions is "Yes," see detailed instructions.

NOTE

Under the law, the "author" of a "work made for hire" is generally the employer, not the employee (see instructions). For any part of this work that was "made for hire" check "Yes" in the space provided, give the employer (or other person for whom the work was prepared) as "Author" of that part, and leave the space for dates of birth and death blank.

NATURE OF AUTHORSHIP Check appropriate box(es). **See instructions**
☐ 3-Dimensional sculpture   ☐ Map   ☐ Technical drawing
☐ 2-Dimensional artwork   ☐ Photograph   ☐ Text
☐ Reproduction of work of art ☐ Jewelry design   ☐ Architectural work
☐ Design on sheetlike material

b

NAME OF AUTHOR ▼

DATES OF BIRTH AND DEATH
Year Born ▼ Year Died ▼

Was this contribution to the work a "work made for hire"?
☐ Yes
☐ No

AUTHOR'S NATIONALITY OR DOMICILE
Name of Country
OR { Citizen of ▶_____
     { Domiciled in ▶_____

WAS THIS AUTHOR'S CONTRIBUTION TO THE WORK
Anonymous?   ☐ Yes ☐ No
Pseudonymous? ☐ Yes ☐ No

If the answer to either of these questions is "Yes," see detailed instructions.

NATURE OF AUTHORSHIP Check appropriate box(es). **See instructions**
☐ 3-Dimensional sculpture   ☐ Map   ☐ Technical drawing
☐ 2-Dimensional artwork   ☐ Photograph   ☐ Text
☐ Reproduction of work of art ☐ Jewelry design   ☐ Architectural work
☐ Design on sheetlike material

3 **a**

YEAR IN WHICH CREATION OF THIS WORK WAS COMPLETED This information must be given ◀ Year in all cases.

b DATE AND NATION OF FIRST PUBLICATION OF THIS PARTICULAR WORK
Complete this information ONLY if this work has been published.
Month ▶_____ Day ▶_____ Year ▶_____ ◀ Nation

4

See instructions before completing this space.

COPYRIGHT CLAIMANT(S) Name and address must be given even if the claimant is the same as the author given in space 2. ▼

TRANSFER If the claimant(s) named here in space 4 are different from the author(s) named in space 2, give a brief statement of how the claimant(s) obtained ownership of the copyright. ▼

APPLICATION RECEIVED

ONE DEPOSIT RECEIVED

TWO DEPOSITS RECEIVED

REMITTANCE NUMBER AND DATE

DO NOT WRITE HERE
OFFICE USE ONLY

MORE ON BACK ▶ • Complete all applicable spaces (numbers 5-9) on the reverse side of this page.
• See detailed instructions.   • Sign the form at line 8.

DO NOT WRITE HERE

Page 1 of _____ pages

EXAMINED BY	FORM VA
CHECKED BY	
☐ CORRESPONDENCE Yes	FOR COPYRIGHT OFFICE USE ONLY

DO NOT WRITE ABOVE THIS LINE. IF YOU NEED MORE SPACE, USE A SEPARATE CONTINUATION SHEET.

PREVIOUS REGISTRATION Has registration for this work, or for an earlier version of this work, already been made in the Copyright Office?

☐ Yes ☐ No If your answer is "Yes," why is another registration being sought? (Check appropriate box) ▼

a. ☐ This is the first published edition of a work previously registered in unpublished form.

b. ☐ This is the first application submitted by this author as copyright claimant.

c. ☐ This is a changed version of the work, as shown by space 6 on this application.

If your answer is "Yes," give: **Previous Registration Number** ▼　　　　**Year of Registration** ▼

5

DERIVATIVE WORK OR COMPILATION Complete both space 6a & 6b for a derivative work; complete only 6b for a compilation.

a. **Preexisting Material** Identify any preexisting work or works that this work is based on or incorporates. ▼

b. **Material Added to This Work** Give a brief, general statement of the material that has been added to this work and in which copyright is claimed. ▼

6

See instructions before completing this space.

DEPOSIT ACCOUNT If the registration fee is to be charged to a Deposit Account established in the Copyright Office, give name and number of Account.

Name ▼　　　　**Account Number** ▼

7

CORRESPONDENCE Give name and address to which correspondence about this application should be sent.　Name/Address/Apt/City/State/Zip ▼

Be sure to give your daytime phone ◄ number

Area Code & Telephone Number ►

8

CERTIFICATION* I, the undersigned, hereby certify that I am the

Check only one ▼

☐ author

☐ other copyright claimant

☐ owner of exclusive right(s)

☐ authorized agent of _____

Name of author or other copyright claimant, or owner of exclusive right(s) ▲

of the work identified in this application and that the statements made by me in this application are correct to the best of my knowledge.

Typed or printed name and date ▼ If this application gives a date of publication in space 3, do not sign and submit it before that date.

date ►

☞ Handwritten signature (X) ▼

9

MAIL CERTIFI-CATE TO	Name ▼
Certificate will be mailed in window envelope	Number/Street/Apartment Number ▼
	City/State/ZIP ▼

YOU MUST:
· Complete all necessary spaces
· Sign your application in space 8

SEND ALL 3 ELEMENTS IN THE SAME PACKAGE
1. Application form
2. Nonrefundable $20 filing fee in check or money order payable to Register of Copyrights
3. Deposit material

MAIL TO
Register of Copyrights
Library of Congress
Washington, D.C. 20559

May 1992—50,000

☆U.S. GOVERNMENT PRINTING OFFICE: 1992-312-432/40,019

FORM CA

UNITED STATES COPYRIGHT OFFICE

REGISTRATION NUMBER

TX : TXU : PA : PAU : VA : VAU : SR : SRU : RE

Effective Date of Supplementary Registration

. . . .
(Month)   (Day)   (Year)

DO NOT WRITE ABOVE THIS LINE. FOR COPYRIGHT OFFICE USE ONLY

(A)
Basic
Instructions

TITLE OF WORK:

REGISTRATION NUMBER OF THE BASIC REGISTRATION: YEAR OF BASIC REGISTRATION:

NAME(S) OF AUTHOR(S):   NAME(S) OF COPYRIGHT CLAIMANT(S):

(B)
Correction

LOCATION AND NATURE OF INCORRECT INFORMATION IN BASIC REGISTRATION:

Line Number: . . . . Line Heading or Description . . . .

INCORRECT INFORMATION AS IT APPEARS IN BASIC REGISTRATION:

CORRECTED INFORMATION:

EXPLANATION OF CORRECTION: (Optional)

(C)
Amplification

LOCATION AND NATURE OF INFORMATION IN BASIC REGISTRATION TO BE AMPLIFIED:

Line Number: . . . . Line Heading or Description . . . .

AMPLIFIED INFORMATION:

EXPLANATION OF AMPLIFIED INFORMATION: (Optional)

EXAMINED BY: . . . . CHECKED BY:	FORM CA RECEIVED:	FOR COPYRIGHT
CORRESPONDENCE: ☐ YES	REMITTANCE NUMBER AND DATE:	OFFICE USE ONLY
REFERENCE TO THIS REGISTRATION ADDED TO BASIC REGISTRATION ☐ YES ☐ NO	DEPOSIT ACCOUNT FUNDS USED: ☐	

DO NOT WRITE ABOVE THIS LINE. FOR COPYRIGHT OFFICE USE ONLY

CONTINUATION OF: (Check which)   ☐ PART B OR   ☐ PART C

D

Continuation

DEPOSIT ACCOUNT: If the registration fee is to be charged to a Deposit Account established in the Copyright Office, give the name and number of Account:

Name . . . . Account Number . . . .

E

Deposit
Account and
Mailing
Instructions

CORRESPONDENCE: Give name and address to which correspondence should be sent:

Name . . . . Apt. No. . . . .

Address . . . .

(Number and Street)   (City)   (State)   (ZIP Code)

Daytime telephone number (. . . . .) . . . .

CERTIFICATION* I, the undersigned, hereby certify that I am the: (Check one)

☐ author ☐ other copyright claimant ☐ owner of exclusive right(s) ☐ authorized agent of: . . . .

(Name of author or other copyright claimant, or owner of exclusive right(s))

of the work identified in this application and that the statements made by me in this application are correct to the best of my knowledge.

F

Certification
(Application
must be
signed)

☞   Handwritten signature: (X) . . . .

Typed or printed name: . . . .

Date: . . . .

*17USC §506(e): FALSE REPRESENTATION—Any person who knowingly makes a false representation of a material fact in the application for copyright registration provided for by section 409, or in any written statement filed in connection with the application, shall be fined not more than $2,500.

. . . .

(Name)

. . . .

(Number, Street and Apartment Number)

. . . .

(City)   (State)   (ZIP Code)

**MAIL
CERTIFICATE
TO**

(Certificate will
be mailed in
window envelope)

G

Address for
Return of
Certificate

▲ February 1991—20,000

☉U.S. GOVERNMENT PRINTING OFFICE: 1991-282-170/20,012

Writers' Rights

This section will define the different rights which empower you to present your work on the market. You should retain as many of these rights as possible. As a beginning writer, you won't be able to negotiate with the editors as well as one who is more experienced. As you acquire more skill, reliability, and professionalism and the more known your name becomes, you will be considered more valuable to the editors. Then you will be able to have an edge as to what you expect for your work.

The following are some of the rights publishers/editors seek from writers for greeting card and postcard verses, magazine article submissions, and photographs or illustrations.

- **All Rights** — These are bought by some magazines and greeting card companies. A writer who sells written work under these terms, forfeits rights of ownership of this material everywhere else. Some editors will work with you, buying all rights for a certain period of time, then letting you recover the rights later.

- **First North American Serial Rights** — Magazine companies which distribute their material to the United States and Canada frequently buy these rights. This lets the company be first to use the material in the U.S. and Canada. The writer still owns all other rights.

- **First Serial Rights** — The company will be able to print the work before anyone else is able to do so. All other rights still belong to the writer.

- **One-time Rights** — The company can use the work only one time, and has no guarantee that it will be first in publishing the material. This right can be used for any kind of material.

- **Second Serial Rights** — A newspaper or magazine has the right to publish material after it has appeared in another publication. The income derived from these rights is usually shared fifty/fifty by the writer and first publisher.

Knowing your rights is very important. This is your leverage in dealing with editors or publishers. You want to be able to be in control as much as possible, so that you can get the full benefit of the knowledge and experience on which your work is based.

Query Letters

As stated earlier, before you send any material to a company, you should send a query letter. This brief letter introduces you and the material you have to offer. Within this letter you should ask for writer's, artist's, and/or photographer's guidelines if you have not had previous access to them. If you send material without permission, you may have it returned or rejected simply because you didn't meet the specific guidelines. It's also possible that the company has gone out of business; find out before you send a costly package. When you receive the guidelines, the best advice is this: follow them exactly. Some publishers require that their guidelines be followed precisely; that's why they have established them for presentation to those who inquire.

A query letter should consist of: the date of the letter; the address of the company; an attention line for a specific contact person or department; indication of why you are sending the letter; your name typed with a space for your signature; your address; and a statement to indicate the enclosure of a self-addressed stamped envelope (SASE). The letter should have a balanced format. In other words, margins should be set so that the letter is centered on the page. If the letter is not centered, let it be a bit higher on the page, rather than too low. A sample query letter follows at the end of this section.

Attaching a brief biography (no longer than one page) is an added touch which might interest a publisher or editor. It should consist of pertinent information relating to the type of material which you wish to submit. Information which is not relevant is likely to cause an editor/publisher to stop reading, viewing the material as useless in evaluating your potential.

Date

ABC Publishing Company
1111 Editor's Street
City, New York 00000
Attention *Editor or department*

My name is Patrisha Stauss, and I am a freelance writer.
I have written various types of greeting card verses. I
am interested in your company's reviewing some of my
work. I would like to receive your writer's and
photographer's guidelines.

I would appreciate any other facts pertinent to making
submissions to your company. Enclosed is a SASE for any
information to be sent to me. Please send the material to
the address below:

Patrisha Stauss
0101 Writer's Lane
Book Path, California

Thank you for your time.

Sincerely,

Patrisha Stauss

Enclosure   sample letter

2

GREETING CARD COMPANIES

Finding addresses and sending query letters are the easiest steps to perform. Remember that the query letter is the beginning of your selling yourself as a professional freelance writer. If you can obtain permission to send your work to a company, you then have the task of impressing upon the publisher or editor the fact that you are capable of meeting her/his standards for making money for the company. Creating that impression will be the deciding factor as to whether you have the talent and experience the company wants.

You may think that you will be able to sell your material to a publisher or editor because you received permission to send your work. Don't get your hopes up until you see a letter accepting your material and stating that a contract or release form will be on its way to you. Although you were asked to send your work, it can still be rejected for a variety of reasons. Remain alert to all of the company's angles and expectations by reading the guidelines carefully, thus decreasing the likelihood of getting a rejection notice.

You should understand the different greeting card categories. If you have this knowledge, you will know what the company is expecting when they mention any given category. In the eyes of the company, it doesn't look good if you appear to guess at what they want. Leaving such an impression is a sure sign of an amateur writer or of one who doesn't care about the company's needs.

There are three categories of greeting cards: traditional, studio (contemporary), and alternative cards.

Traditional Cards — These cards have been around for a long time. This classification addresses events and wishes such as birthday, wedding, get well, sympathy, Christmas, Thanksgiving, Easter, Mother's and Father's Day. The verses in these cards have a generalized meaning, yet they are expressed with a sensitive and emotional feeling.

Studio (Contemporary) Cards — This category of cards is the same as the traditional set, but the verses are somewhat different. These poems or passages are geared toward the changing of the times. They have a specific meaning with a message that is non-traditional (a more involved meaning). If you write in this area, pay close attention to what is being sold on the market. What may have been popular last year, may not be so this year.

Alternative Cards — This series of selections includes thank you, promotion, salary raise, divorce, friends, gags, and other non-traditional cards with off-beat or humorous messages. This category is rapidly growing in popularity.

Not only do you need to know the card categories, you also need to be aware of the company's clientele, both buyers and receivers of the cards, *e.g.*, woman to woman, mother to daughter, son to father, friend to friend. When the company has specific guidelines in the particular areas, you need to pay special attention to those requirements for your submission. Many card companies will send you samples of their card line if you request them.

You may have specific ideas about the way you would like to present your material, but the publisher knows what she/he wants to sell. The company guidelines will show you what is expected of a writer; you decide to follow them or not. Don't take the chance of losing the opportunity to work for a company just because you may not like the guidelines. The publisher or editor knows that there are many writers who will comply with their standards. If you like a particular company or if only a few have answered your query letter, then rearrange your work or style to fit the company guidelines.

Contacting the Company

In order to contact greeting card companies, you must know where to get the addresses. You should be prepared to spend some time researching the market, determining which company would fit your needs (or which ones have needs which you can fit). Below is a list of places and a description of what you should look for when you have located a good source.

Book Stores — There are a few books which specialize in supplying addresses for a variety of companies. Before you buy a book, be sure that it has addresses for greeting card companies. If that category is not listed on the front or back of the book, check the Table of Contents. The more information the book can supply you, the more you will benefit from using it. Here is what you should look for in determining if the book can be of use: 1) company name; 2) company address; 3) contact person; 4) whether the company will consider the work of freelance writers; 5) what writer's rights they want to obtain; 6) submission time or deadlines for acquiring material from the writer; 4) the company needs and product lines; 8) tips for the writer; and 9) how to contact the editor.

Libraries — Your library may have the telephone yellow pages of various cities throughout the United States. In the yellow pages, look under the section of either publishers or greeting card companies. This may be of some use, depending on the city. Not all cities will have a listing for greeting card companies. The phone book listing will not have the ZIP code, so you will have to go to the post office to obtain ZIP codes for the addresses you have obtained.

Local Stores — Many stores sell a variety of greeting cards. On the back of each card you will find one or more of the following: the publishing company's name; city, state and ZIP code; and/or the phone number. Sometimes the cards may be on a rotating stand with a sign on top advertising the company which produced the cards. This advertisement may have the company address.

Magazines — Magazines geared toward the business of writing will have many advertisements near the back cover. Usually there is a section for greeting card companies which need writers. Here they will mention what type of material they seek, and the address will be included.

After you have obtained all of the company addresses, prepare a query letter (see page 20). It is advisable to put an attention line on the outside of the envelope. After you send the letter, you can expect to wait up to six weeks before you get a reply. Some companies may not answer your query letter, or you may get the letter returned, unopened, because the business no longer exists.

When a letter has been returned to you, first check to see if you have enough postage on it. Then compare the address on the envelope to the one you have listed in your files. You will be able to see if you accidentally wrote something incorrectly in the address. If you made a mistake, readdress the envelope and send it on its way. If the letter was undeliverable, keep it for your records. A discussion pertinent to this matter can be found in Section Four.

The Publishers/Editors

If the greeting card company has specific guidelines, its editor will expect the writer to follow them. It is to your benefit to do so, or you may lose the opportunity for your work being accepted for the market. The guidelines may state that the company pays a flat fee. Another bit of information may be regarding what types of rights the company may buy. Such facts will give you an idea about how to approach the company's publisher or editor, or about how the company may approach you regarding payment.

Companies differ with regard to acceptance of unsolicited material. Some will review it; others may look it over; quite a few won't review it at all, but will send it back if you have a SASE enclosed.

If you sent your material to a company for review after receiving permission to send it, and after a reasonable period of time you haven't received a reply regarding its status, write a letter inquiring about it. Don't bother trying to call, because you may not be successful in reaching the person who has direct contact with the material. In fact, it is unlikely that you would be able to speak to the publisher or editor. These people are very busy and usually have others helping them with their mail and phone calls. A letter will be more beneficial, for it will allow time for determining the status of your submission.

Once your work has been accepted for sale on the market and you are at the stage of revising or finalizing your material, a publisher or editor will welcome your phone calls. Your phone call will definitely be accepted if you run into problems while working on the specific material requested by the company.

When your submission has been accepted, you should receive a letter stating such. That letter will indicate any further requirements that may be expected from you, in addition to the work which you have already sent to the company. You then must decide whether you still want to work for the company. If you do, send a reply letter stating so. You will receive a contract which may be negotiable, depending on the determination of the company and the stance of the publisher or editor. The company's belief in the marketability of your product will determine how far it will negotiate with you. The more reputable you are, the greater your edge in negotiating. For all the company knows, someone else could be competing for your work.

Be careful not to be too stubborn regarding your expectations; you may lose out.

Selling Your Rights

Keep as many of your rights as possible. In some cases, a writer may have little say about the rights sold to the publisher or editor. If a beginning writer says, "No," too many times, he may find himself out of the range of being on the market with that card company. A publisher or editor knows that there are many writers who will comply with the company's requests; they may not want to bother with one who won't "go along."

The best way to decide what rights you should sell is to take a look at your material and determine if and how it may be resalable with other products on the market.

If you sell all rights or your copyright, you can terminate the transfer of rights forty years after the sale or thirty-five years after publication, whichever comes first.

Make sure that whatever you do with your rights, the agreement is presented in writing. Be sure you understand the terms that an editor or publisher is offering. If the offer is not put in writing by the company, you should present your understanding, in writing, to the publisher or editor. Remember that there is sometimes a turnover in such positions as publisher and editor, and the rights purchased may change, too. An agreement should be stated in writing to prevent any such changes.

A PROFESSIONAL APPROACH

The professional approach requires, in addition to the elements previously discussed, a professional manner in presenting your material. Since this step will be the final deciding factor for your work to sell, you need to be sure that the material is compiled as though it were your finest work ever.

Any piece you send to a publisher or editor should have your own style, unless the guidelines don't give you the opportunity to do so. Think of an eye-catching format which you would like to present. Put yourself in the chair of someone having to review the material. Try to be objective about your work.

Whenever you have the chance, add designs or artwork to your material. Many card companies will state in their guidelines whether they would consider photographs or any other artwork. The specific requirements would then be stated. If the company supplies its own illustrations, try to get examples of its work so that you can produce your written material according to the style of its card line.

Before and during the time you critique your work, check for errors and make any other changes that you believe are required. After you have completed any piece of work, critique it as though you were going to market it yourself. You will want to be as strict as if it were someone else's work. The best test you can put on yourself is to decide if you would buy it. If the answer is, "No," go back to the drawing board.

You can expect some "rejection" or "not interested" notices. This may not be a reflection on your work, especially if the company hasn't reviewed it. There are several reasons why your manuscript may not be accepted. Some of them will be discussed in a later section.

Do not get frustrated and ready to quit because of a few rejections. Everyone goes through this, and everyone can learn from the experience. If your work is returned without being reviewed, send it to another company. If it has been reviewed and rejected, you have two alternatives: 1) send different material to that company, if the rejection letter invites you to do so; and/or 2) send the same material to another company which has indicated a willingness to review your work.

The Writer's Style

Now I would like to help you develop a style or improve your techniques for formatting your material. I shall give you some ideas as to how you can look professional to any publisher or editor.

Your first step is to check the guidelines to see whether the card company wants you to be specific in submitting your verses or passages. Once you have met their specifications, you can add your touch of professionalism.

The guidelines will vary depending on the preference of the company. Below are some possible expectations from a company regarding the writing aspect of your submission.

3 x 5 or 4 x 6 Index Cards — Type one version on the top half of the card and your name and address on the bottom half. At the top right corner, place some kind of code for your reference and record keeping. Place your copyright notice at the bottom left corner. If a photograph or artwork is to be included, tape it on the back side of the verse.

Specific Card Line — The type of cards sold on the market could be listed. Examples are: birthday, get well, miss you, congratulations, and holidays. This area is important to know because any verse that does not fit the company's needs at that time will be rejected immediately. If a deadline for submission is stated, mark it on the calendar. Don't miss it. Otherwise, you can forget sending further submissions to the company for that year.

Style of Verses — If the company only wants humorous verses, don't send them something sentimental. Many companies will send you examples of their types of verses. If you send them something they do not market, it's a sure bet that it will be rejected. Look to see if the guidelines state the categories of buyers on which the company focuses (such as women to women or friend to friend).

Other Product Lines — This line includes: mugs, buttons, tee shirts, calendars, post cards, note pads, stationery and bumper stickers. Your verses may be used for any of these items. Sometimes the company may feel that your verse would be more suitable for one of the above rather than for a greeting card. On the other hand, your verse may be suitable for both the greeting card and another product line.

If the guidelines have not stated a specific format, I suggest the following:

On a 8 1/2 x 11 piece of paper, type one verse centered. On each sheet, type your name and address on the top left side of the sheet with your copyright notice on the bottom, placed either on the left or right side. It is wise to put some kind of code on the top right side of the page for your reference and bookkeeping.

The code you use should be apparent to the category or type of verse.

You could use any one of the codes below. These are just a few examples; you can easily make up your own.

H 15 = "H" stands for humorous; "15" stands for the verse written.

S 25 = "S" stands for serious; "25" stands for the verse written.

R 10 = "R" stands for religious; "10" stands for the verse written.

XMAS 2 = "XMAS" stands for Christmas; "2" stands for the verse written.

MOM 6 = "MOM" stands for Mother's Day; "6" stands for the verse written.

When you have compiled between ten and fifteen verses, clip them together and send them to the greeting card company. This number of verses will give the editor a variety of ideas from which to choose. The company may accept one to all of the examples to review for the market.

Before you submit your material, read and incorporate the following to make the verses look professional.

1. **Paper** — Use quality paper, not erasable bond. If possible, print on a soft tan or gold color paper. Never send your work on paper that is torn, wrinkled or mutilated. Be sure that the paper is clean of unwanted marks.

2. **Ink** — Whether you use a typewriter or a computer, be sure that the ink is dark and the printing is even. Black ink is preferable. The letters should be legible and un-smeared.

3. **Print Style** — Study the style of print for the companies you would like to send your material. If a company seems to like a variety of fancy print, try to send them something unique. Some companies prefer standard print; to these,

you would do well to send them exactly that — with minimal changes in print style.

4. **Verse Length** — Some companies will prefer a particular length for their verses. If the guidelines do not mention this, take a look at the cards sold in stores. Stay close to the company's preference. State, if needed, which part of the verse should be on the outside and which on the inside of the card.

5. **Other Product Lines** — If you would like to use your verse on another product line instead of in a greeting card, you should state this in a letter with your submission. It is best to have these verses separated from the greeting card verses if you are sending them at the same time. Be specific as to how the verse is to be printed or presented on the item.

6. **Error Free** — Always look over your verses at least three times. This is a precaution; you may see an error you overlooked in the previous review. Read cautiously. Publishers and editors know that everyone can make a mistake, but some extremely noticeable errors cannot be overlooked.

If you are conscious of all of the areas above, applying some, if not all, you will have a good chance of receiving a publisher's and/or editor's positive response toward your work.

Using Photographs and Illustrations

If you have other artistic talents — such as photography or illustrating (computer graphics or artwork) — and you would like to use them with your verses, this subsection will hold valuable information for you. Before you send any piece of artwork, be sure that the company has stated its approval in the guidelines. It may be better for you to send your artwork without a verse to a company. That's permissible if the company will accept it.

Let's assume that the company would like to see your artwork. Be sure to place your copyright notice on your material. The following are some specifications which a company may want to see.

Photographs — Camera ready is preferable. The photograph will be accepted in one or more of the following formats as stated in the guidelines: slides/transparencies, color prints (various sizes), black and white prints (various sizes), contact sheets and negatives (upon request only). If a caption is to be used on the photograph, there should be enough space to provide it. If a theme exists, a notation on the photograph should be provided.

Illustrations — Camera ready is preferable. Have the work geared toward a specific design, season or holiday. Card specification for the artwork may be mentioned as well as the type of paper preference. Finished artwork might have to allow for bleed where appropriate. If illustrations are cut and taped or pasted on the paper, copy it and check for any shadows that will need to be covered; then correct and recopy the sheet.

If words are to cover part of a photograph, be sure to provide enough space (*e.g.*, open sky area or off-center of the subject to the right or left). The space in the photograph should be either a light or very dark color. Black ink can be printed on the light colored area and white ink can be used on the dark area. If you want to use colored ink, it's best to do so on a dark area in the photograph.

When a person is a specific target or the main subject in a photograph, you will need a photo release form signed by that person, giving you permission to use it for sale. An example of a photo release form is presented on page 34. You can change some parts of the release form, but remember to keep most of the wording. There are specific legalities which apply to the way the release form is stated.

A photo release form will protect you regarding any suits from the person who is in the photograph. By law, you need his or her permission in order to sell the photograph on the market.

When you have taken a photograph and a number of people happen to be in the background, don't worry about the model release form if their faces cannot be distinguished. These people were not the main subject of the photograph; they just happen to have been caught in the camera lens.

To prevent your work from getting lost once it reaches the company, it should have your name, address, phone number, an ID code for reference and your copyright notice displayed in one of the following manners.

- **Greeting Card Verses** — On 3 x 5 or 4 x 6 cards, place the information on the front (preferably) below the verse. If you don't have room for it on the front, place it on the back; it will still be acceptable. If you choose the latter, note it in a letter to the company.

- **Individual Greeting Card Verses** — On an 8 1/2 x 11 paper, you can present your information in one of two ways. Present the information on each sheet (front or back), or staple all sheets together and attach a cover letter with your information.

- **Multiple Verses** — If you want to take the time and have access to a binding machine, you can bind the cards or the sheets of paper containing the verses. With this format you should place your identifying information on the front cover. I advise that you send a cover letter with the package.

- **Photograph Book** — If you would like to get more elaborate, you can place your work inside a photograph book, displaying your identifying information on the front cover. Don't use an album which might make it difficult for the publisher/editor to take out the material.

- **Photographs** — Put all your information on a 3 x 5 card and tape it to the back of the photograph.

- **Artwork or Illustrations** — Place your identifying information on the back of the sheet. If the writing would show through the paper, you should write the data on a 3 x 5 card and tape it to the back of the sheet.

Patrisha Stauss
0101 Writer's Land
Book Path, California
(916) 111-0000

MODEL RELEASE FORM

In consideration for value, I _____, do hereby give Patrisha Stauss and parties designated below, the irrevocable right to use my name and photograph for sale to and reproduction in any medium for purposes of advertising, trade, display, exhibition or editorial use.

If any other companies, purchasers, agencies or licensees wish to use my name or photograph, further permission needs to be requested from _____.

I have read this release and fully understand its contents. I affirm that I am more than 18 years of age. Permission of name and photograph usage is designated to:

_____

_____

Witness: _____Signed: _____

Address: _____Address: _____

_____

_____

Date: _____Date: _____

GUARDIAN'S CONSENT

Since _____ is under 18 years of age, I affirm that I have legal right to issue consent as stated above.

Signed: _____ Date: _____

Critique Your Work

Now you have printed your work so that it is appealing to the eye, formatted it for a professional look, copyright protected it and given it a style all its own. Is it complete? Have you gone over it thoroughly enough that you believe it is definitely ready for the market? Are you ready for someone to review and critique it professionally? Can your work compete with other material on the market? If you say, "No," to any of the questions above, you must critique your work more thoroughly.

The critique of your work (by yourself) will pay off for you financially. The publishers and editors will appreciate your effort. It saves them the time of correcting or reformatting the work. The publishing company saves money when less time is needed to compile the material.

Keep in mind that to critique your work is to look at every aspect of your freelance business, not just the work you produce. When your material is positively ready to be presented to publishers or editors, you should be able to answer, "Yes," to each of the questions in the first paragraph above. Now ask yourself the following questions.

1. Will the card company consider the material as fitting their product line?

2. Will a publisher, editor or anyone buying the card understand what is being conveyed?

3. Is the typing and context legible and error-free?

4. Does the material fit the company guidelines?

5. Is the format uniform and consistent?

6. Would I buy my own material?

7. Am I aware of the kinds of rights the company wants to buy?

8. Does the artwork or photograph fit the written material?

9. Does the artwork or photograph fit the company's guidelines?

10. Does the artwork or photograph look professionally done?

11. Is the material coded for record keeping reference?

12. Is the quality of the work acceptable for sale on the market?

13. Did I copyright the material?

14. Does the material look original?

15. Have I looked over the material enough times to say, "Yes," to all of the above questions?

There may be times when you feel that no one could resist your work, yet you get a "rejection" or "not interested" letter. There are a variety of reasons for that kind of response. Don't take the rejection of your work as a personal rejection; see what you can do to make the next submission more acceptable. Before you get upset and want to quit, check all the possible reasons below.

- It's supposed to be a humorous card, but it isn't funny enough.
- The verse doesn't make sense.
- The idea has been overworked.
- The verse is too corny or too cute.
- The material doesn't fit what's being sold on the market.
- Guidelines weren't followed.
- The artwork isn't suitable for the type of verses being written.
- The deadline for the material was missed.
- The company wasn't accepting new material at that time.
- The company doesn't accept unsolicited material.
- You may have asked for the material to be used on a product the company doesn't produce.
- The publisher or editor has changed, and the material may not fit the requirements of the new person.
- Your expectations could not be met.

KEEPING WORK ORGANIZED

The signs of a sound business are good organization, up-to-date filing and accurate record keeping. I have a three-level system for my record keeping process: 1) I have addresses of all the material or letters that I have mailed (the contact person and the company phone number are also listed); 2) my ledger has the company name and the date of any material which I mailed or which was returned to me; and 3) I have records on accounts payable and receivable for all transactions which involve money.

Not only is being organized a good idea for your benefit, the government will also be interested in your financial situation. When it's time for you to compute your taxes, the government's interest should be in your mind; if they receive any records of your transactions from other sources, they will be expecting to hear from you. The more organized you are, the more efficient your record keeping procedure will be. This will enable you to spend more time on your freelance work. The way you process your transactions and receipts will be important to your record keeping system.

You should keep track of all your transactions in the form of a filing system, whether it is on a computer or in a filing cabinet. If you are able to use both a computer and a filing cabinet, one can be used as a back-up to the other.

The supplies you have on hand are also a part of staying organized. It could be very frustrating and time-consuming if you don't have the items on hand when you need them. You could also miss a submission deadline if you have to take the time to make a trip to the store.

Imagine that it's Thursday night and you are preparing a submission which should arrive at a company on Monday or Tuesday. To have it ready in time, you need to mail the package on Friday. If you do not have the items you need to complete the work on Thursday night, you now have to go to the store on Friday, finish the work, and still try to mail it before the end of the day. If you have to work at a regular job, you may have less time to get all of that done. Try to keep on hand all of the items you will need (or extra, if possible) for every aspect of your writing or artwork. The more accessible these things are, the more effective you can be in meeting deadlines.

I always keep more than enough work material on hand, so that I won't discover that I don't have enough of something to finish a project. When I see that I am getting low on an item, I purchase more than needed at that time. I suggest that you periodically check your supplies or keep a running list of what is needed. Such a list will prevent you from forgetting what to buy when you arrive at the store.

You should be aware of the type of mailing services which are provided for you. If you know what mail services exist regarding prices, amount of time needed for delivery, how the service is provided, what preparation is needed, and office hours, you can choose the best type of service for sending your material. A company may have suggested a particular mailing service which it would like you to use. If you are more aware, you can save time because you planned ahead.

Record Keeping

I will describe to you my method of record keeping. Then I will give you some other ideas which you may want to incorporate into your own method of record keeping. I use a computer and a filing cabinet to store my information. Because I am a very organized person, I believe I can give you some good advice about how you can become well organized or better organized. I will describe my three-level system and explain, step by step, how I stay organized.

Within my writing area, I have a "basket" which consists of material to be filed, that which requires more work, incoming and outgoing mail, items I have to read, and anything which requires photocopying. Any time I receive something related to my freelance business, I look at it immediately. At that time I decide whether or not to place it in my basket. If something needs my attention at that moment, I take care of it; otherwise I put it in the basket. I check the basket once a week to file the material and enter information in the computer.

If I receive a rejection notice, I treat it like a normal letter to be filed. It's filed and noted in the computer and on the hard copy as a rejection notice. I don't want to send any information to the same company twice. Businesses don't appreciate that type of mishap.

Computer Filing

Addresses — This category has different subcategories (related to areas of writing) which list the particular addresses of letters or material which I have sent or received. After each address, I indicate the contact person and the company phone number. The subcategories are: "Poetry Publishers," "Greeting Card Companies," "Magazines," "Children's Book Publishers," and "Minibook Publishers." When I list the addresses, I write some kind of notation or a symbol to remind me that I have mailed or received something. I use the symbol (#) for noting that I sent a query letter and the symbol (*) that I received something. Any other information

I may need to know is placed next to the symbol in parentheses.

A Ledger — This is a form which has the following information at the top of each page: company name, description of item(s) sent, date item was mailed and returned to me. When I send my card verses (or any other material), I place the information in the ledger. Each page of the ledger has the name of the month during which the activity occurred. Remember that if you have any material returned to you, make the notation within that month. Below is a short example of the appearance of the form.

Ledger - Page 1

(June 1992)

Company Name	Description	Date Sent	DateReturned
Card Pub	HG 1,4,7,8	13	

Ledger - Page 2

(July 1992)

Company Name	Description	Date Sent	DateReturned
Card Pub	HG 1,4,7,8		26

Accounts Payable and Receivable — This is another form related to the ledger, except that it shows transactions involving money. The months on this form can be combined unless you have many activities occurring in the same month. It is important to keep these records so that you will be able to keep track of your expenses and the money you receive. In the beginning of your business you will not make a profit. When you do begin to make profits, you will want to know.

If you are not familiar with the terms *Accounts Payable* and *Accounts Receivable,* read the following definitions.

Accounts Payable — Money which you pay someone for his or her services.

Accounts Receivable — Money which you receive from someone buying your material.

ACCOUNTS PAYABLE/RECEIVABLE MARCH - JUNE 1992

DATE	ITEM	COMPANY	AMT PAID	AMT RCVD
3/18	Card Illus.	Bill Rase	50.00	
4/10	5 Cards	Love Greetings	250.00	
5/29	Article	Kids Poetry		42.00

Once all the information is entered in the computer, I will do one of two things depending on how hectic my day is. If I have a slow day, I will file the hard copies in the file cabinet. Remember that some of the information will stay in the computer and will not be printed. If you have a computer hard drive, save it there and on a floppy disk. The disk will be your back-up copy. If I'm too busy to file, I will put the information back into the basket and work on it later. You will have to decide how to manage your time. Don't let the basket get too full or let too much time pass before you get to it. Waiting too long may cause you to miss a submission deadline.

File Cabinet

A file cabinet should be arranged in alphabetical order by main categories. Within the main categories, you should have subcategories alphabetized. The following are the main and subcategories which I have in my file cabinet.

Main Categories	Subcategories
Artwork	Borders
	Holiday Design
	Illustrations
Business Addresses	Card Companies
	Magazines
	Printers
Copyright	Copyright Information
	Blank Forms
	Forms Completed
Correspondence	Letters Sent
	Letters Received
Greeting Card Co.	Company Information
	Form Letters
	Guidelines
	Publishers/Editors
Letterhead	N/A
Minibooks	Book Publishers
	Form Letters
	Work in Progress
Miscellaneous Info.	Book Information
	Printing Co. Info.
	Self-Publishing
Photography	Agencies
	Articles
	Companies
	Form Information
	Photography Info.
	Release Form
Poetry	Articles
	Company Info
	Contests
	Form Information

Receipts

Writing

Artwork
Equipment
Miscellaneous
Photography
Writing

Articles
Form Letters
Company Info.
Publishers
Writing Information

Organizing your time will allow you to be more efficient and not miss submission deadlines. I have a calendar on which I mark the deadlines for my submissions. The calendar can have information regarding the stages of the work (including completion) which I wish to have accomplished by specific dates. I check the calendar daily or weekly, depending on the type of assignments on which I am working.

Sometimes I may have ten items to accomplish in a weekend. I write them on a piece of paper and cross them off as I finish each one. I may number the items on the list and work in sequence.

Other Ideas

If you don't have a computer, you will definitely need a typewriter. Get an electric one with correction feature. You will have to type one of each form and make several copies. Have enough space on the form so that you have room to type everything. Some typewriters have a spell check, but you still have to read every word and every sentence carefully. Do this more than once. Often I will see an error which I missed the first time through. Before you send the material to anyone, check the ink quality and formatting, and have it error-free.

If you can't afford a file cabinet, you could use a sturdy box. Use manila folders to divide the categories and subcategories. There is no way around it; you will need a filing system. When the companies begin responding to your inquiries, the filing will accumulate. You will find that many companies are willing to answer your query letter. Never throw away the letters (even rejections); file them so that you are aware of your status with each company. Don't throw information in a box without some organization; save yourself the frustration of having to search through everything for one small piece of information.

Try to find a small bookcase or a table with shelves to hold your material. I like the idea of a bookcase. Besides holding books on it, you can put such items as paper, envelopes, folders, and scissors. All your material should be kept in the same area, so that you don't have to hunt for anything. The secret is to be organized for efficiency.

You should always use top quality material. Don't settle for second best. It's better to spend a little more money for quality than to lose an assignment. Some companies may like your writing, yet reject your material because of poor quality in a photograph or artwork.

Some writers get someone else to shoot their photographs or illustrate their work, because they do not have the time or cannot do the job as well as a professional in that field. The best professional for you to use as photographer or illustrator is one who is a friend or relative who will wait for his or her pay until you get paid.

Remember to record who helps you with any part of your work. You don't want to forget whom you have to pay and how much. You could develop a contract which both of you will sign. The contract is proof of what the agreement is between you and the other party.

Preparing Your Submissions

Don't think that all you do is put your material in an envelope and mail it. That simply isn't so! Some company guidelines state the way in which you must submit your work. If there aren't any guidelines, you could follow the techniques below. (SASE means self-addressed, stamped envelope.)

- Whatever the size of your submission, *always* send the company the same size envelope with the correct postage for return. Always keep three sizes of envelopes handy: 6 x 9, 8 1/2 x 11, and 9 x 12. Don't forget to write your address on the stamped return envelope.

- Query letters may be folded and sent in a #10 envelope. If you are expecting the company to send you information, be sure to send them an 8 1/2 x 11 envelope with enough postage.

- Send all your material by First Class mail. That rate will be handled more carefully than Third Class. You will pay more, but it's worth it.

- If you have a thick submission, you could place it in a box not much larger than the material. Place your SASE inside the box.

- To send photographs or slides, pack them well and try to send them with the submission. If you have to send them separately, include a cover letter stating exactly what goes with what. Both submissions should be coded for easy matching by the person receiving the mail. Photo mailers can be bought to hold the photographs for better protection. Slides should be put in plastic sleeves and packed between card board or in a small photo mailer. If you want them back, state in your cover letter that you would like to have the photographs returned. Don't forget the SASE with the correct return postage.

- If your submission is mailed out of the United States, you will have to add extra postage to send it and to have it returned. Some countries will want you to send International Reply Coupons (IRC); check the guidelines. You can obtain IRCs at the post office.

- When photographs/slides are being mailed, write "Photos — Do Not Bend" on the outside of the package. This alerts the postal people and the receiving company to be careful when handling it.

I learned the hard way. When I started mailing my

photographs, I put them between two pieces of paper. I was very upset when they came back to me scratched and bent. You can prevent this by following the directions above. I've found that companies respect your request that material be returned when you send a SASE. Be sure to write your return address on envelopes and packages to ensure their return in case the company has moved or is no longer in business.

Mailing Services

There are several different ways you can mail your submissions:

1. **First Class** — This is regular mail service. Although it is the most expensive way to mail, it generally receives better handling and is delivered the quickest.

2. **Third Class** — Not as expensive as First Class. The delivery takes longer and the handling by the postal service is rougher.

3. **Fourth Class** — This rate is usually used for packages and is handled very roughly. Be sure to pack slides or photographs in a sturdy photo mailer within the package.

4. **Certified Mail** — The letter or package has to be signed when it reaches its destination.

5. **Registered Mail** — This service is expensive, but it assures careful handling and high security. The item is signed in and out of every post office. The receipt is then returned to the sender once it reaches its destination.

6. **Air Mail** — It's very expensive, but delivery could be there the next morning or afternoon, depending upon when the plane leaves for that destination.

7. **United Parcel Service (UPS)** — This service is somewhat cheaper than First Class. Any letter you send with the submission, must be put inside the package. UPS cannot legally deliver First Class mail. The cost depends on the weight of your package and its destination.

8. **Federal Express** — This is an overnight service. This, too, is an expensive way to mail, yet it is guaranteed to get to its destination the next morning (or the next afternoon) within a wide mailing range.

9. **International Mail** — You will have to add extra postage depending on the country to which you mail it. Ask your local post office. You may have to use an IRC, because U.S. postage would be useless.

From the above types of mail services, it is likely that you will use First Class, Third Class or International IRC. The other services would most likely be used or requested by a company after you've begun working for them.

5

THE PROCESS OF WRITING

Now you can begin the actual writing process. There are three ways to present the writing to be placed on a card: 1) a few lines on the outside and a few on the inside; 2) one or two lines on the outside and the rest of the verse inside; or 3) the whole verse on the inside of the card. If a photograph is on the outside or inside, remember to leave space for the writing (if needed).

Photographs and illustrations should be used to represent the verse. Therefore, you may have to place your verse according to the space available on a photograph. You will also need to be careful that your photograph isn't overbearing or out of proportion for the size of the card.

You should try to place the writing toward the top half of the card because that portion of the card shows when it's in the store rack. Most people will look at a card if it is eye-catching; reading the verse comes after that.

Don't force yourself to write. When the words are ready to be expressed, you'll know, because your thoughts will flow easily. There have been times when I had to motivate myself to write by placing myself in an inspiring environment. This will be discussed later.

After you have compiled your work, critique it objectively. Don't be too hard on yourself, yet critique the material honestly. If you feel unsure about what you have done, don't submit it to a company. It's better to miss a deadline than to submit incomplete or lesser-quality material.

After researching the card market and studying the contents of this book, you can begin your freelance writing. Have all the items you need at hand, then find the right place to write and let it flow.

Getting Prepared

Before you begin writing, I would like to suggest some inspiring environments.

1. Sit near flowing water or a lake; nature's sound can create a calming effect.

2. Remain in your home playing your favorite record, compact disc, or cassette.

3. At night, find a place to overlook the city lights.

4. Sit on green grass in a park or at a college campus.

5. If there is a particular subject you want to write about, put yourself in a similar environment for inspiration.

6. Try to imagine a particular situation or event.

7. If you have pictures/photographs depicting a certain situation, examine them while trying to imagine being there.

8. Talk to someone about your particular subject in order to get mentally aroused.

Some writers may get a mental block and find it hard to write within any of the above situations or places. If you find this to be true, don't force the writing; wait for a better time.

Verses

The following information will help you to better understand and visualize how verses are used for greeting cards.

- Look at the next few examples and notice how they would be placed on a card.
- Verse writing can be considered a good opportunity for a writer's self-expression. You can use the opportunity to express a message of particular inspiration. The message needs to express a common feeling, because people buy cards to express what they feel or would want to tell someone. Keep this in mind. If there isn't a meaning in the verse, the card will not sell.

Long verses should have the first part on the outside of the card and the rest on the inside. The following two examples would be too long to have the whole poem placed only on the inside of a card. You should write a note to the publisher, or make a diagram as I have, showing your suggestion about placement of the verse outside and inside the card.

Example 1

Outside
of
Card

Through the hustle
And bustle,
Through the rush of life,
Clocks are standing still
For no one.

As we battle to
Stay on the move;
Hopes often vanish,
As clocks keep us on the run.

As time steadily ticks on,
We're never knowing the
Moments left behind.
Passing through life without
Taking a glance.
Through the turmoil
And the chaos,
We could lose the meaning
Of it all.

Do we dare take that chance?
For time stands still for no one.

Example 2

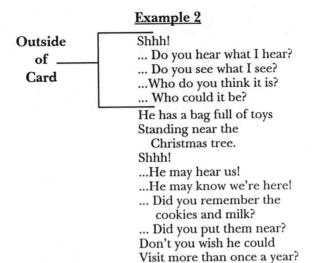

Outside of Card

Shhh!
... Do you hear what I hear?
... Do you see what I see?
...Who do you think it is?
... Who could it be?
He has a bag full of toys
Standing near the
    Christmas tree.
Shhh!
...He may hear us!
...He may know we're here!
... Did you remember the
    cookies and milk?
... Did you put them near?
Don't you wish he could
Visit more than once a year?

The following examples are short enough (yet not too long) to be placed inside a card. You may use these verses as shown.

Example 3

Outside or Inside of Card

You are part of my life
As is the sun and the stars.
You brighten my days;
You give me security at night.

You are my star,
When my world seems dark.
When I feel I cannot go on,
Your nearness shines over me,
To help me through my somewhat
Times of nothingness.

With you I know the sun will shine.

Example 4

Outside or Inside of Card

Santa, Santa, he's on his way,
Bringing gifts
    On Christmas Day.
Happily bringing lots of toys
For all good
    Little girls and boys.

Yes, Christmas night is
    Growing near,
And jolly Saint Nick
    Will soon be here.

Another type of verse writing is considered a short verse. This type of verse will always have one or two lines on the outside and on the inside of the card. The outside lines will begin the verse, and the inside lines (of the card) will complete the verse. When you send short verses to the companies, mark them as done in the following four examples.

O) = Outside of Card   **I)** = Inside of Card

Example 5

O) Getting married will be a promising moment...

I) ... Be careful the moment isn't too short.

Example 6

O) So, you're retiring soon...

I) ... Now maybe you'll get some work
done around here.

Example 7

O) I'm sorry to hear you're in the hospital.
Don't worry about the bill...

I) ... The doctor keeps a running tab.

Example 8

O) Let me know if you need any help at any time...

I) ... Just give me at least a week's notice,
since I'm very busy.

Some companies have a preference as to what type of verse they want, and some are open to a variety of ideas from freelance artists. Be sure you know what the company has stated in its guidelines.

Passages

A passage is best kept inside a card. It is used for cards other than the traditional kind. In other words, they are used as inspiring words for nontraditional cards such as best wishes, graduation, promotion, and going away. Look at the examples below.

Example 1

Are thoughts enough to take you
where you wish to go?
Well, I guess if you don't try them out,
you will never know.

Example 2

Things are how they are
but that's not how they must be.
Close your eyes
and open your mind and
maybe you will see.

Example 3

Careful how you make your plans.
Once life actually stagnates,
you may never have the strength
to make it gain momentum again.

Example 4

Try as hard as you will
to get what you want.
But by all means,
be thankful for what you've got,
because some might not have *that much*.

Passages are usually meaningful segments taken from any written work or from your own thoughts; as such, they can and will vary greatly in length and structure. Passages on the average are rather short; it would be unusual to find passages more than twelve lines long. There are few rules to writing passages; they can rhyme, but need not; they can be one line or many; and the subjects are limitless.

Each passage can be used to store portions of personal thoughts and quotes from other works which you have produced. You may also find that writing your own passages for commercial purposes can be very rewarding. Passages can be copyrighted and sold. They are widely used for tee shirts, drinking mugs, bumper stickers, buttons, and stationery products. Many passages can be used to teach, entertain, warn, or persuade. With passages, you can write as little as you need, to say as much as you want.

≡
≡

6

TAX INFORMATION

If an area of your home is used only for business, you may deduct the expenses on your income tax. You need to have an income of $400 or more within one year, in order to file. You will have to pay self-employment tax, separate from federal tax.

You are to declare the income on the federal income tax form. The law requires a business make a profit three years out of five years before it is considered a business and not a hobby. You will have to contact the IRS to discover whether you can claim a loss within the first three years of your business. Save receipts for all expenses. You will find many items you may be able to deduct on your tax form. The tax form changes yearly; be sure to check if the following are deductible for a given year. You may find that you can deduct more than what is on the list below.

paper	typewriter material	business-related books
utensils	camera equipment	repair services
gas mileage	car usage	postage
artwork materials	travel expenses	envelopes
computer hardware	photocopying costs	printer costs
or software	stapler/staples	business-related seminars

Don't throw away receipts. Place them somewhere, filed and organized, for easy access at tax time.

The more accurate your records are to balance with your receipts, the more valid they will be for tax use.

7

CONCLUSION

Every technique and advice in this book is what I follow to be a successful writer.

Writing verses of personal, political, emotional or spiritual expression can be used in greeting cards, magazines, mugs, tee shirts, buttons, calendars, minibooks, and bumper stickers. All you must do is choose which area interests you and then engage your talents, experiences and positive attitude.

After you have critiqued your work, you could have others do the same. This would be a good opportunity for you to hear what others think about your writing. When someone critiques your material, treat it as constructive criticism and learn from their opinions. Ask how they might have written or presented what they have examined. It doesn't hurt to listen to suggestions about different ways of presenting your material.

If you can reach others through your writing, consider your efforts worthwhile. When people buy your material, they are expressing their approval. They are also telling you to keep on writing and displaying your artwork.

INDEX

ABOUT THE AUTHOR

Patrisha Stauss received her Special Education Credential in 1983. Between 1981 and 1989, she taught both children and adults with a variety of learning disabilities.

In 1987, while teaching, she began freelance writing. Using her education, teaching experience, and research skills, she wrote as a hobby. In 1988 she co-authored her first educational book, *Poems and Passages.*

Several of Patrisha's poems have been published. She is currently writing educational curriculum, how-to and self-help books, and supplemental educational books.

In 1989, Patrisha decided to leave her teaching career and use the realm of writing to teach others. Through her books, she hopes to decrease the level of frustration felt by many.

Additional copies of

FREELANCE WRITING FOR
GREETING CARD COMPANIES
by Patrisha Stauss,

may be ordered by
sending $12.95 postpaid
for each copy to:

DISTINCTIVE PUBLISHING CORP.
P.O. Box 17868
Plantation FL 33318-7868
305-975-2413